The Purpose Ladder

Valentina Quarta

Copyright © 2022 Valentina Quarta

All rights reserved. No part of this publication may be reproduced, distributed, or transmitted in any form or by any means, including photocopying, recording, or other electronic or mechanical methods, without the prior written permission of the publisher, except in the case of brief quotations embodied in critical reviews and certain other noncommercial uses permitted by copyright law.

Paperback ISBN: 9798446022069

First paperback edition 2022

Edited by Advyth Herur
Cover art by Massimo Quarta

Printed by Amazon.com, Inc.

Independently published via Kindle Direct Publishing

kdp.amazon.com

to Canel, who reminded me that I can
to you, who need the same reminder

"In the midst of the winter, I found there was, within me, an invincible summer. And that makes me happy for it says that no matter how hard the world pushes against me, within me, there's something stronger, something better, pushing right back"

– Albert Camus

Dear Reader,

This book is a love letter to the child at the bottom of your eyes, who imagined you'd go full force after your dreams when you have longer legs and bigger feet. And yet finds you racing from task to task, from mail to mail, from post to post, quite unsure about who picked for you the destination you're rushing towards.

We procrastinate the most on becoming who we've always been. As children, we already know our truth, but we spend all our adult years chasing it back, invested in the lengthy process of unlearning what others want us to look like, inside and out.

In a constant attempt to avoid failure, we tend to forget that we can fail at something we are not fond of, so we may just as well try doing what we love. At times, however, even when we resolve to follow our passions, we are rather indecisive about what they entail. So loud is the noise both off- and online that we have forgotten the sound of our own voice.

Answers like to hide in the silent quiet of self-discovery. We insist on looking for them in articles, talks, and gurus' words, but the more we search for them outside, the deeper they get buried within. Eventually, we realize that *self-awareness is our first step home*. And we pray for this to be a step towards our favorite bookshop or our best friend's house, then frown when we discover this is a step outside the comfort zone instead. It is the beginning of a journey in which our ability to learn from fear, failure, and pain becomes the navigation system through the maze of our untapped potential.

From breakdown to breakthrough, we let self-awareness restore our power to become the architects of our minds and create a more fulfilling life. This architecture, we notice along the way, is not one of addition but one of subtraction of the layers of social and cultural conditioning. It's one of balance between being and becoming. One in which we fully embrace our authentic selves and feast on the joy of being accepted and loved for who we are. It's an architecture of purpose in which we create meaning by putting our passions at the service of our fellow beings.

On this path, authenticity may feel lonely at first as it often comes at the cost of old relationships and dynamics, but only when we show up as ourselves can we attract the people that are meant for us. How would they otherwise recognize us while we are wearing a mask?

I know that many things along the way have not gone according to plan and that this may make you doubt your deservingness and enoughness. However, remember that our thoughts are self-fulfilling prophecies, what we believe we attract. And sometimes, we may be wrong about what we think we want, which is why there are only three possible answers to our aspirations: a) yes, b) not yet, and c) the universe has in store for you something better that you can't yet conceive.

Despite all those disappointments, look at you, here you are, enjoying the chance to breathe another breath and dream another dream. And I hear you objecting that dreams are fluffy things but flip your hopes into plans and watch "one day" become "day one." They tend to laugh at dreamers yet try and laugh at dreamers with a plan.

From nothing to something to everything, this book starts with my story and ends with yours. It will take us from the victim mindset of "things happen to me," through the growth mindset of "things happen by me," to the aligned heart-set of "things happen through me."

It's never too late to become yourself, and my job is to remind you that you lack nothing.

Love, Valentina

Part I - Nothing

Beginnings

Note to Self

You feel stuck in a rut. Like you are constantly trying to take steps towards safety and fulfillment, but the finish line is taking steps too. The more you walk, the less you arrive. You aren't yet ready to acknowledge that saying that you're stuck is a victimizing statement, trying to hide the fact that you still enjoy the comfort of familiar discomfort. Staying in the known, even when it is painful, seems easier and less effortful than embracing change and the challenges of the unknown.

You tell yourself that you are waiting for the right time. Yet your brain is designed to like what is familiar: It will never naturally feel like the right time to revolutionize your mental, emotional, and physical habits, not without an active effort to choose the uncertainty of the unknown.

The Body

The body knows what you'd do
if you realized you have a choice
It can feel how you jitter
while nodding with great poise

The body knows the traumas
you conceal as never happened
it knows about the abuse
the sense of guilt you carried

The body hears you say
'I got this, I can, I'm strong'
and knows you really think
you've done everything wrong

The body knows you're staying
in a relationship you have outgrown
it knows you're only staying
because you're scared of moving on

The body knows that meds
cure symptoms and not causes
The body knows the words
you never tell your parents

It knows you think you're late
and wish to ignore its timing
that you follow others' schedules
instead of self-aligning

The body whispers that
which you must find out
if you refuse to listen
it will begin to shout

Receiving

Note to self

You have forgotten how to receive. Most of us grew up with punishment as an ever-lurking shadow. Its script recites that if you do something wrong you will or should be punished. Our teachers, parents, and certain religious circles have gladly ensured that we internalize the script. If we did something bad we were bad.

You would think that now that you are an adult, you are well past this mind trick. Unfortunately, the conditioning of punishment is so ingrained in the adult brain that because there is no one around to punish you, when you make a mistake or do anything less than perfect, you subconsciously punish yourself. What once was a "you were bad, so no candy" becomes a "you were bad, so no money" or "you were bad, so no love". You sabotage your success to ensure abiding to the punishment script. Your guilt blocks your growth. This makes you bad at receiving, for how could you be possibly deserving of life's goodies when you are constantly making mistakes and being imperfect?

Vicious Cycles

Judging others = a need to be superior

A need to be superior = feeling deeply inferior

Feeling deeply inferior = expecting love and validation to come from the outside

Expecting love and validation to come from the outside = relying on the judgement of others

Uncoupling

Note to self

What do you get out of playing the victim? Attention. Why do you live for attention? You have made the critical mistake of confusing attention with love.

Craving attention leaves you at the mercy of others. You will find yourself engaging in people-pleasing behaviors and taking decisions for the sake of validation and positive reinforcement (even when they are in misalignment with your core values).

It is necessary for you to uncouple attention and love so you can begin loving yourself and others for who they are and not for what they do for you.

Belonging

If you think that stars are far apart
look at how much further we are
from the people around us
who don't see or acknowledge us
for whom we truly are

Narratives

Note to self

You are psychologically incapable of predicting what will make you happy and fulfilled. Your deductions are based on models and examples surrounding you but bear no certainties. You mistakenly believe that getting what you want equals fulfillment hence every time that you don't you mourn and suffer.

In truth, however, when things don't go the way you want them to, you don't miss out on something that would make you happy, you only miss out on something that you *thought* would make you happy, something that you perceive as desirable.

Since you couldn't recreate what you perceived as desirable, you don't celebrate what *did* happen to you. You are blind to the goodness of your current circumstances simply because they don't fit your made-up narrative about happiness.

Burnout

We miss-punctuate life
since we stopped using semicolons
our days too fast-paced
pauses are time that feels stolen

We jump from comma to comma
on the to-do lists in stock
till the body halts in a burnout:
an inkless pen's full stop

Worthiness

Note to self

Success is associated with getting and becoming more. Yet contentment is about the capacity to appreciate what one already is and has.

You don't need to feel worthy to become successful. Some of the wealthiest people in the world have very low self-worth and that has been their main drive for accomplishment: Their achievements are the result of a need to prove themselves, and their efforts are trauma-driven.

Yet while unworthiness won't keep you from getting successful it will keep you from feeling content because it will prevent you from appreciating who you are and what you have (no matter how much that is).

Navigation

There is no GPS to navigate
the path to our truth
only an internal compass

Yet we are misrouted
over golden bridges to shopping malls
built to deliver promises of enough
and keep our dreams small

Band-aids over amputated limbs
we close our eyes and pray
that buying instead of being
will fill the emptiness away

Procrastination

Note to self

Much of your suffering resides in the gap between knowledge and action, between what you know you should be doing and how you choose to spend your time, between what's right and what's easy. You widen this gap by digging up reasons not to execute and identifying problems that all so suddenly must be attended to before you can proceed.

Quickly, the gap between knowledge and action turns into the trenches of a war with yourself. The only white flag you wave is the bright surface of a screen, which does nothing other than ensuring further procrastination.

The solution that you're resisting is to reflect less and experience more, to concentrate your efforts on living not on thinking about living.

Self-Doubt

I sit on a beach
but I'm not on vacation
I'm one of the sand corns
still I'm told I'm special

maybe they say that
so I buy more of what they sell
I'm one of the many sand corns
I don't know why I'd yell

louder than the others
like I have something to say
I'm just the stranger in my mirror
it's to this dry land I obey

Northless

Note to self

Your compass is northless, your luggage full of limiting beliefs. You feel like the only way of finding a way is to follow others, imitating their success. Yet copying others' "happy" often leaves you stressed out and dissatisfied. There is only one rule: find out your core values and live in alignment with them. But at this point you don't understand this predicament, you have gathered too little experience and shiny objects still blow the wind in your sails.

You are busy asking everyone about truth. You just want something to believe in, something to hold on to. You haven't yet internalized that humans are too unique for magic bullet solutions. No coach, book, course, or guru can teach you your truth. Uncovering it comes from tapping into knowledge buried within, not without. It can't be outsourced, not even from an article that starts with "Scientists at the University of X found that..."

Reading empowers you. It is the act of shedding light on questions no one taught you to ask. However, you still can't see that everything you'll ever read bears the same lesson: Don't do things by the book unless you're the author.

Imposter Syndrome

You say you are self-conscious
when you mean you are conscious
of others being conscious of you
You say you fear others' opinions
when you fear what you think
that others think about you

It is all false narratives
that you became convinced about
the imposter is not you
it's the mind that makes you doubt

The Ego

On the way to the beach, I met my ego. She said, 'I'm the holder of your beliefs about yourself and the world. I help you make sense of this human experience on earth. I'm the voice inside your head, but I'm not yours. I'm the internalized voices of those around you as you grow. My job is to protect you from pain, but if I'm wounded and you're unaware, peace will be a trophy you can't attain.'

I asked how I'd know if she was wounded. She replied, 'I'm very iffy and I have a lot of ifs. If when growing up, you didn't feel safe or were pushed to be something you were not. If you were not allowed to express yourself or were shamed for your emotions and traits a lot. If now your beliefs are inflexible and you hold too tightly to some identity. If you think too much and feel too little, and you see a threat in those who think differently. If you over-compare yourself to others, try to win approval through achievements and prestige. If judging, shaming, criticizing to feel valid are a recurrent trick up your sleeve.'

Perplexed I continued, 'So you're telling me I'm stuck with a voice in my head that's not even mine and filters and shapes everything I decide?' She nodded, 'Unless you become aware of my wounds and how they affect your behaviors and truths. You can begin by acknowledging your thoughts and paying attention to how you interact with the world. As you observe, you can begin to change, make conscious choices, create new responses, and start speaking in your own authentic voices.'

Paper Dad

As a child, my grandma had only seen her father in a photo and came to believe that he was made of paper. Other girls could hold their dads' hands while all she had was a wrinkled black and white image on a thin sheet. My great-grandpa had been held prisoner during World War II and only managed to return home when his daughter was ten years old.

On the day of his arrival, the villagers decided to gather several girls about my granny's age and let my great-grandpa guess which one his daughter was. He stood in front of the smiling crowd and without hesitation pointed at my grandma, 'That's my child!'

Beaming with pride, my grandmother felt chosen by her own parent for the first time. She realized that her dad wasn't made of paper and that she'd be able to hold his hand after all.

However, the fear of separation and abandonment never really left her. Every time a family member leaves the village to go on travels, she cannot conceal the terror that departures awaken in her heart.

I wonder how many of the wounds of our forefathers are passed on to our skin, how much trauma our genes carry that we never directly experienced, and how many more things we must heal from that we know nothing about.

Shadow Selves

Note to self

The things you love about others are the things you love about yourself. The things you hate about others are the things you can't accept in yourself, the so-called "shadow selves": those bits of you that you were conditioned to believe were not okay. It's the parts that you suppressed and did your best to stop acknowledging.

When you meet someone who embodies these parts, you feel negatively about them. This is not because you dislike these bits but because you are fighting your desire to integrate them into your life.

Loneliness

I tried to fit in many places
and always unsuccessfully
until 'Who am I?' became
'What's wrong with me?'

I attract people who feel
empowered to be by my side
if they're down I lift them up
if I'm down I must lift myself up

The only one catching me if I fall
is my dirty kitchen floor
if being human is connection
then I've done this all wrong

Until I hear a soft voice
innocent, pure, warm
she tells me that I'm loved
and that she'll never leave me alone

I skeptically ask, 'Who are you and what's the price?'
She says, 'I am the child at the bottom of your eyes
If you connect to me, to our truth at its core
I promise you, you will never be alone

'We deserve to be acknowledged and seen
and independently of other people
I'll do it for you, you do it for me'

The Waiting Room

Head in the i-clouds
where perfect is the new normal
please like, comment, and follow
validate my transit through this portal

A slot machine of information
intermittent variable reward
causing legal addiction
procrastination on what is hard

In the meantime, a stream flutters by
carrying opportunities untried
singing of natural landscapes
of love, adventure, and fire

'What are you going to do with your life?'
the stream asks daily
'While chances keep streaming by
I'll go on scrolling waiting to die'

Anxieties

My anxieties are selfish
so I must help them see
what happens when "me" and "I"
turn into "us" and "we"

No Screens Attached

We shop for love in apps, selecting humans like clothes. We scan for the minutest flaws and swipe away from our carts everything that doesn't fit our narratives. We don't settle, we want the best, yet are never quite sure about what that entails. We feel entitled to the perfection that fairy tales promised and the media reinforces daily. No one seems to notice that fairy tales haven't been fair at all: They told us that they lived happily ever after but never revealed how.

The main goal of our texts is to seem busy and important. Instead of providing attention, we want to look like we don't care and so stir the perfect repellent potion to send the other on their way to the next swipe. Someone must text first, as long as that's not us. We want to seem cool and not reveal weaknesses despite knowing that vulnerability is the way to deep and meaningful connections. Unfortunately, we don't appreciate imperfections even if that means we don't appreciate ourselves.

Sometimes we hide behind the excuse that we are practicing self-love when in fact we just want to stay in our comfort zone and not face the complications, insecurities, and emotional hurdles that relationships reawaken in us. At other times, we simply want some quick validation and attention, a breath of fresh air for our ego.

We believe that the screen protects us from accountability and so feel free to be less tactful. We don't end things, we ghost, we disappear. We are nice people so why tell ugly truths when others can figure them out by themselves? We will let them hope, we remain sure that they won't shed a tear. And even then, it would be a quick wipe and swipe. The shopping spree begins again and maybe the next item will fit our expectations better.

Avoidance

The largest part of your discomfort doesn't come from pain but from your hopeless attempts at avoiding pain. Surrender to your pain and watch it shrink.

The Clock

Note to self

When will you stop being obsessed with the idea that you're too late, that the time to do what matters most to you has elapsed? This sense of "all ships already sailed," of "I've watched the sand in my hourglass slip by"?

Don't you see that it is an excuse? Don't you know that people have become award-winning actors in their fifties, best-selling authors in their sixties, parents in their forties, and so on? The world has given you plenty of proof that there's no such thing as "too late," yet you choose to hold on to the lie. You must not want it enough. Do you want it enough? Then re-set your watch. It's not two o'clock, it's *you* o'clock.

Who Am I?

Note to self

What if my purpose comes to me in a foreign language and I don't understand it?
How do I know which one of the voices in my head is my authentic self?
What's the right answer when the mirror asks, 'Who am I?'?

Part II – Something

Potential

There is an invisible world at the crossroad of your thoughts
made of all the decisions you never dared to take
and all the projects you parked in front of a red light

In this world, all street signs point inward
away from the crowd, toward your authentic self
where freedom is more than a word

In this world, you're reminded that
your potential has no shelf life, it doesn't expire
yet when unexpressed, it turns into pain
as you miscall "impossible" what you never tried

In this world, no time is better than now to try
to make the invisible world visible to the naked eye

Passion

They ask me, 'What is your passion?' The answer is, 'I have forgotten,' because I didn't get to practice it. I'm not surrounded by like-minded others. And on days in which I remember, my passion feels like an untamable being, placed so far outside my comfort zone that I'm not sure if I dread or enjoy it.

My idea of "possible" is biased by the old, that the future must fit in the past's same mold. They say that I should hold my passion's hand each day, slowly let it feel again like a friend. That she's inevitable, she's not a trend, that she knows me better than anyone can. They say, 'You may race faster alone, reach the peak of mountains and domes, but she'll take you much further, much deeper into yourself, your home.'

The Power of Yet

You feel like there is so much more to you than you allow anyone to see. There is a sense of untapped potential hosting all the selves you could be.

'But I know so little, and I'm so small,' you shrug and sigh, 'I wish I was a bird, but I don't know how to fly.'

The grand oak tree you're leaning against interrupts you with a whisper, 'Little human, you're forgetting a word, the one you put in the end but serves to begin it all. Instead of complaining about not having this or that, consider harnessing the power of "yet."

'You don't know how to fly yet.

'You don't know how to love yet.

'You don't know how to be successful yet.

'The things you can achieve expand indefinitely when you stop making plans based on what you already know and begin relying on what you can learn as you grow.'

Courage

I want to be like a strawberry
the fruit of all fruits
that wears its seeds outside
bravely, fiercely
proud to show its essence
first things first

Renewal

I bend over the lake, and my reflection asks
'If you could be anything, what would you be?'
After heavy-lidded pondering I say
'If I could be anything I'd like to be me'
'And who is this you that you'd so want to be?'
'Someone living halfway between becoming and being'
'What about those thoughts and feelings
that you carry in shades of blue?'
'They're the ink but I'm the writer
each day I write myself anew'

Awareness

Note to self

Your body is a house you decorate and redesign. You pick chandeliers for your ears, different shadows for the curtains of your lids, you shape the rooftop with hairstyles, and paint the front door with lipstick. You wrap the exterior in branded clothes so the neighbor knows what you can afford. Yet your attention is so oriented outward that this is a house you can never move in. You hang in the garden from the ego tree.

Then one day, the stronger wind of adversity lashes against you and blows you off your comfortable branches. Covered in dirt, you begin realizing that understanding oneself is what turns a house into a home, that the unaware are banned from their own abode. You notice that when you try to grasp what you are without attempting to change or embellish it, what you are transforms. This transformation, however, is not based on appearances, it moves from the inside out in a constant strive for alignment. You grasp then, that awareness is the key to the door back home, to feeling like you belong within your skin's walls.

Un-Layering

As children, we can't lie
nor be other than who we are
just like in the rest of nature
a tree is a tree, a star is a star

Then grown-ups punish us
for telling the truth to others
and our innocence is gone
we deceive sisters and brothers

It becomes a habit
we lie and forget why
until one day we wonder
'If not this, who am I?'

We are told to become someone
trade peace for self-promotion
the child knows they are someone
like rain is rain, an ocean an ocean

We are told to emulate
trade uniqueness for conformity
the child knows to go their way
their only strive is for simplicity

To keep alive the child within
shout to someone what's true
innocent and open and simple
and it's fine if that someone is you

Excuses

I sat at a table with Time, Authenticity, and Humility.
'I'm late on the schedule of my dreams,' I complained aloud.
'I will keep on passing whether you work on them or not, so you may just as well start now,' Time ticked and tocked.
'But who will pay attention? Who will believe my story?' I protested.
'People believe the message when they believe the messenger,' Authenticity beamed, 'Live your truth, walk the talk.'
'Yet who am I to make my voice louder than others and claim things for myself?' I wailed.
'Don't set out to take. Set out to give. It's not you or others. It's everyone co-elevating everyone else,' Humility smiled.

Beliefs

Note to self

I can see how on some days you seem afraid to be happy and look for things that could go wrong. You find those and attract them. And there you sit comfortably in your pain because it's familiar. You pat yourself for having predicted outcomes correctly when all you did was write self-fulfilling prophecies against your dreams.

They say it loud and clear, we don't see the world as it is, we see the world as we are. Our reality is the result of a prediction based on past personal history and current beliefs. And you can't change your past but what are you going to believe? Only what you sincerely believe can be predicted and manifested into existence. Even epigenetics – the science that studies changes caused by the modification of gene expression – shows that what we believe can alter our genetic makeup.

Some people with serious illnesses believe that they have a contribution to make to the world, so they recover and move on. Others believe that their life is worthless and die. Some people believe that they will be successful and innovate, so they do. Others, who may be more gifted and exposed to fewer difficulties, believe that they can accomplish nothing and so they don't.

What are you going to believe?

Attention

A spider had been strolling outside my window for days, or so my roommate says. On a Monday, I saw the spider too, and my light arachnophobia made me stare at it in horror and wish it was gone. I closed my eyes and prayed for it to move its business somewhere else. When I peeked through my half-opened lids, the spider, that had spent a long while outside the window without bothering anyone, had suddenly entered my living room.

Such is the power of attention. When it comes to unwanted things, the key is not to wish them away as much as it is to not direct our attention toward them. The wise say that where attention flows energy goes, and we attract that which we are interested in. Dwelling on negative emotions magnifies them. The answer is not to wish these emotions gone as much as it is to turn attention away after having witnessed them. Acknowledging the spider and then going about our day.

I wonder what would happen if we were to begin focusing on the idea that there's a conspiracy for greatness in our lives.

Pacing

We find validation in our busyness
yet busy lives are empty houses
everything fast-paced is unwise
wisdom is savoring time as it passes

I tuck my child at night and don't say
'Have sweet dreams' but 'Have big dreams'
not chasing shiny objects, instead
resting down the eyelids and gazing within

Essentialism

Note to self

Don't commit before exploring. Most things in life are unnecessary noise. Do not commit to the first interesting opportunity, this too may be nothing but empty buzz. Try out several options. Exploring more of the world outside will take you deeper within, and going deeper within will teach you what matters to you in the world outside.

When it comes to action, practice the art of doing less but better. Remember that most things are not worth your time and energy. Progress is not made by doing more, it is made by doing fewer unnecessary things and concentrating on your essentials.

What matters to you? Focus on it to the exclusion of all surrounding distractions.

Resilience

Mother nature doesn't complain
about compost and excrements
it turns them into flowers

Resilience II

I work out and my body is fatigued
yet given ample time to recover
it comes back stronger than before

The same is true for the mind
when it undergoes the workout
of challenging times

Mindfulness

There is nowhere to arrive
breathe in, say "here"
breathe out, say "now"
you have arrived

On the next breath again
you have arrived
the scenery already novel

Presence

Why do you long for beauty
even whilst you swim in it?

You're in Rome and dream of Paris
get to Paris and miss the sea
but if you can't be here and now
there's nowhere else you can be

Gratitude

If you keep looking for happiness
you tell yourself it's not there with you
if you were to count your blessings
you'd see you don't need something new

You woke up this morning
while someone somewhere didn't
time passes as a warning
don't postpone the joy of living

Thank the universe for being here
you could have been nothing or small
yet you were chosen as a wave in this sea
as impactful witness to the magic of all

Journaling

I open my journal
and start singing along
later I realize
I never turned the music on

Along what am I singing then?
Maybe music is how I sound
when I lower the volume
of everything around

My journal asks that I unload the grind
let concerns out of my system
every single drop
so they belong to its pages
not to the mind's internal blob

The journal keeps asking
as the ink glistens:
'What's the sound of your voice
when no one else listens?'

Vulnerable Self-Talk

Note to self

Strength is the ability to talk honestly to yourself.

You remark the importance of surrounding yourself with people with whom you can be vulnerable and authentic, speak feelings as they are, even the soft ones. But what about vulnerable self-talk? You grew up with an extreme sense of self-reliance so all you can say when a difficult situation occurs is 'I'm fine. All is good. I can power through this one too'. That's what you always did. You are strong and carry burdens alone. Yet the body gives away your lie. You are not fine, you simply haven't learned how to acknowledge and express negative emotions. You've been thinking that strength is a matter of toughness, shrugging away loss and defeat as if nothing was the matter. But what if strength were the capacity to talk honestly to yourself?

Pep talks to build yourself up are helpful. Just as helpful is to make space for negative emotions and listen to their message before they claim that space in the body and later bubble up in illness symptoms. Stop saying 'I'm fine,' when you're not. It may feel like weakness at first, but as long as you don't dwell on negative feelings, you can learn much from them and watch them put you back in your seat of power.

Connection

You didn't come here to be alone
solitude is a rose, loneliness its thorn
you weren't alone from the very start
hosted in a womb, cherished in a heart

You evolved to live in groups
to increase your chance of survival
when you have others to count on
your happy hormones are higher

You were designed to thrive by touch
of both the body and the soul
and this may come as much
from a friend, a tree, a song

The deeper you go within
where all ice melts
the deeper you'll touch
everyone else

Beauty

When you take a picture of a sunset and it doesn't look good you don't say, 'Eww the sky is ugly.' You know it is the camera that can't capture the beauty of the sunset.

Yet when you take a selfie and it doesn't look good you very quickly say, 'Eww, I'm ugly,' when in fact it is the camera that can't capture your beauty.

Heritage

My feet come from far away
from paths I've never walked nor strayed
as my ancestors were tweaking their moves
so they'd fit today in my shoes

My hands held multitudes of babies
carried water and pains and rubies
as my ancestors were shaping their hues
so they'd fit today in my gloves

I'm made of now and many worlds past
DNA letters my forefathers sent
for me to read and send forward at last
to keep our footprints on mountains and sand
our torch flaming over skies and land

The letters tell stories of wars and errors
maybe Rome was built by my predecessors
or maybe they enjoyed the quiet of farm life
family and cattle their idea of empire
As for the genius and the art to enquire
perhaps it's my forebear who discovered fire

So when I feel aimless and left on my own
I recall my ancestor's letters
and bring our footprints
to new treasures and shelters
knowing I never do it alone

Direction

Thunderously the metro enters the central station and plays the soundtrack of progress. The soundtrack of people racing, without really knowing where to.

I get in and out. High-rise buildings block my access to the sky as I look up the way we always do, obsessed with results to achieve and destinations to arrive. This causes me to stumble on a hat, the wallet of the street artist performing at the corner, whose music is muted by my noise-canceling headphones.

I apologize and move on, still looking up, continuing the inner mumbling about goals. Before I know it, I am swallowed by the city center and lost in its maze.

Lighting suddenly, a thought suggests that I can't find my path by solely looking up. I must look to the ground where my feet meet the earth and further below, where my roots enliven my efforts. Direction is spending time to understand our core values and beliefs – our roots – and acting in alignment with them. When watering our roots, we learn that only that which has ground and stability can branch far into the sky.

I take off my headphones and follow the sound of the street artist's music back to the station. This time I sit on the sidewalk and let her drums knock on my heart's door to pick it up for a dance.

Direction II

Have you ever heard a seed complain
it's too full of dirt to shine
to sprout into the heights it takes
to be the tallest pine?

Like the seed you and I
embody the chance to live free
yet of all the available options
we insist on choosing plan B

But concentrating on what we're afraid of
sends it soon knocking on our door

Then how about setting the antenna of our radio
to be receptive to the best-case scenario?

The Unknown

My dreams come true each day
in a place called the *Unknown*
I ask for directions to it
they say it's outside the comfort zone

The road is but a grassy meadow
and at its entrance is a shadow
it glues to your every step
its name is fear, it looks like mirror

Friends warn me away from the Unknown
'It is unsafe, it is forlorn'
yet I must go each day anew
for it is there that dreams come true

The Unknown II

Note to self

Open questions are closed treasure chests hiding jewels we can't yet fathom. They are opportunities to live the answers one by one, trial and error. Do you feel like there is still much uncertainty surrounding your love life? Your purpose? Money? Spiritual growth? Fearful of the unknown, you mistakenly believe that the chests are there for you to carry, when in fact they are only there for you to open. Embrace the undiscovered and the unsettled with the curiosity of the child, looking forward to the surprise.

Why would you rather have nothing to look forward to or wonder about? Don't you know that everything set in stone is already dead? Tonight, rest in gratitude for the answers you still don't have. And don't hide behind the excuse that you might be too old to catch chances in a whiff. You knew all along that the middle letters of "life" are "if."

The Truth about Fear

Such a madness to fear fears
don't you know stars started shining
because they were afraid of the dark?

You think you start too small
to reach for the sky
but don't you see the mighty oak?
It was once just a seed

And I know courage is always hiding
in the last place you look
yet keep looking
don't be overwhelmed
by the intricacy of the woods

There is comfort in getting lost
there is growth in new ways home

Just don't make it your sole concern
for your desires to be met
let me tell you
there's no real happiness
on the other side of that

The Truth about Fear II

Fears are like old friends
we may sit down and listen
to their concerns and advice
then still take our own decisions
as friends never have the full picture

The Truth about Fear III

Lips sewed by fear of judgment
who was I to offer solutions?
My voice mere sound pollution

Until I gathered the courage
to ask the trolls of insecurity
why they condemn so fiercely
why they act with superiority

They said
'If you plunge your blade first
it'll be their blood mixing with dew
If you criticize others first
they won't be able to hurt you'

So I learned that those
keeping me from sharing my love
were the ones who needed it most
the ones with an insecure rove

Meaning

Humans need meaning to live a fulfilling life
they search for it in the safety of their home
yet find it often hiding outside the comfort zone
like to hug one's mother one must leave her womb

As the prowess and attractiveness of youth fade
they recognize that meaning comes from the inside
after proving themselves to others in charades
they stop seeing meaning in ego and its pride

Not all searches for meaning require a revolution
but all require a chat with one's own dust
a choice for what their compost will turn to
a garden full of flowers or more blades of rust

Sometimes meaning is appreciation
for what one already does and has
Most often meaning is an expression
of one's way to serve and share

Self-Love

In my room hangs a portrait
of my ideal self
worshiping it gives me direction
yet the more I dwell on it
the less I appreciate
my own reflection

I look in the mirror and rush to alter
all that doesn't resemble the portrait

I don't seem to understand
I'll never look like the portrait
if I don't love myself for who I am
that self-love is a journey
not a destination
practiced along the way
not at the end station

What am I folding myself for?
Flaws are creases
that can only be filled with love

Time to release
this struggle to please
stop whispering when I should shout
to turn the wish to blend in
into eagerness to stand out

Self-Love II

Imagine if trees wore concealer
cause they don't like their reflection in the lake

If the sun didn't show up at dawn
insecure to rise after scrolling her night awake

Imagine if the sky used the Juno filter
to make itself look paler and smooth out imperfections

If earth went online shopping for clay masks
to cleanse its pores and other obstructions

Imagine birds attaching engines to their wings
to fly higher and faster, leaving trails in our springs

And now think about the child at the bottom of your eyes
about all the other children that you expect to grow wise

Do you really want to tell them this is all about their looks?
Maybe after some scrolling put their nose into books

Compassion

In the vast wide world, I bumped into another creature and shared, 'I'm happy to live and sad to die.'
She nodded, 'So am I.'
I went on, 'I get things I don't want and lose things I want and suffer.'
She nodded, 'I have the same hassle.'
After a pause, I continued, 'I didn't mean to be unkind being blind to your pain. I had forgotten we all suffer the same.'
She smiled, 'When I understand myself, I understand you. When I forgive you, I forgive myself. We borrow needs from each other, nothing we have we own. Resting in this knowledge, we won't suffer alone.'

Patience

A sudden touch on my shoulders
the beaconing of dawn light through trees
I halt at attention like soldiers
I turn around, see you staring at me

Though I promised not to fail you again
there's days I don't think I can
What's a human without a friend?
What is paper without a pen?

You smile at me like in that picture
as you prepared for your first day of school
its sacredness that of a scripture
you were always the wise, I am the fool

You handed me your dreams
you consigned your trust and your hopes
to your dismay as it seems
all I did was tie them in ropes

I beg for more time to grasp our essence
and carry out all your advice
Thank you so much for your patience
dear child at the bottom of my eyes

Forgiveness

Eyes closed I look into yours
I hand you a flower for peace
I forgive you for hurting me

I untie the chains of resentment
and set us free from this energy
I'm not your victim, you're not my enemy
nor permanent marker on my destiny

I allow myself to tap into my potential
reinvent my reflection in lakes
embrace the goodness that awaits

Forgiveness II

Wounds on the skin leave a scar. Broken bones heal without leaving a trace instead. When I am superficial, I hold on to grudges. I reinforce the upset each time I glance at the reminders of those hurts on my skin. But when I go deeper into myself, into the boundless reservoir of love, I see no bitterness nor rancor. There are no scars on bones.

Negative Emotions

Negative emotions are messengers
delivering urgent news
from faraway lands
you lost contact to

Don't shoot the messengers
they are gardeners
bringing tears to water
the seeds of a new you

Failure

I failed so often I lost count
my recurrent meal entailing
mouthfuls of dust from the ground

Each trial ending with a blow
my music playlist reduced
to the sound of the word "no"

And I failed my way into success
there was no other trick
nothing more nothing less

Where fear of judgment abides
from the comfort of our couch
nothing changes nor provides

Let's encourage children to fail
show them the how and why
they'll only really fail
if they never even try

Strength

Standing on a sidewalk on a drizzle-scratched afternoon my father pointed at a little daisy emerging from a crack in the asphalt against all odds. It had claimed its space without accepting excuses and was bouncily sipping from the sky. 'Do you see that daisy?' I nodded. 'That daisy is you,' he smiled his proud smile.

I believed him. And that made all the difference.

Quitting

Quitting is for winners
leaving the job you hate
that toxic relationship
it's never too late
they'll call you sinners
but quitting is for winners

Flow

Note to self

When an activity provides an extrinsic reward – a reward that comes from the outside – you will eventually become used to its benefits and your motivation to practice it will wane. On the contrary, when an activity provides an intrinsic reward – a reward that comes from the inside – you become unstoppable. If you work as a consultant in exchange for a high salary but don't enjoy your tasks, your motivation to consult and contentment in the process will reduce as you become used to your salary and its benefits. On the other hand, writing is an activity that you'd be doing anyway even if no one would ever pay you for it. Consulting brings you an extrinsic reward, writing an intrinsic one.

Intrinsically rewarding activities are the ones that feel like a necessity. You cannot fail in them because failure is measured by outward recognition and these activities are never pursued for approval or applause. They are fulfilling regardless of outcomes and make you lose track of time and hunger. These activities make you become one with the process, and that is good, as the process is all there ever is.

What is something that absorbs your attention entirely and brings order to your chaos? What is something that, even if you were to never be acknowledged for, you would still be pursuing because it feels inevitable? And how can you make more space for it in your life?

Comparison

My love
why do you always take the blame for being late
on imaginary timelines that societies create?
You think everyone around you is on time
besides you, you're stuck drawing outside the lines

My love
why do you call yourself selfish
for keeping distance from people
who dimmed your light?
Why do you carry the shame
for the things you broke
when running from your demons at night?
Why do you think you're at fault
if there's some more layers under your skin
if your nose isn't straight
your thighs not so thin?
Can't you see this is not you lacking
but you being pray to the race
to the scarcity mindset that comparison creates?

Did you know that if you ask someone
to rate their happiness
after having looked at magazines
with unrealistically perfect models
their happiness drops
no matter their morals?

Did you know that if you ask someone to rate
how attractive they find their partner
after having looked at those models
they find their spouses less attractive
no matter their morals?

How can you think your shoulders
are too small to carry big dreams

yet deem them broad enough
to hold the fault for all these things?

Stop

And I don't mean stop comparing at all
cause that's something you can't always control
Your mind won't ask for your permission
to look around and create works of fiction

But if you can't tell the mind to stop
comparing against each cue
at least you can tell it what to compare to

Change your reference points, change your environment
unfollow that account, stop watching that show,
there's no one to keep up with, in your heart you know

Float around those who make you feel inspired
and not like something with you isn't right

My love
it is no stranger in the mirror, it's you

You have eyes, a portal to wonders, your unique twinkle
don't tell me all you can see is the crow's feet wrinkles

You have a mouth that gives you a voice to flip scripts
don't tell me all you can see is the size of your lips

My love
I want you to try one simple thing
toss the phone you're holding, the laptop, or any screen
in fact keep them, let them go on standby
and in the darkness of the screen
look at yourself in the eye

I want you to tell her

'Thank you for holding my life
thank you for trying your best each day
even when you don't know better, you try

'Thank you heart for beating
even when I don't remind you to
thank you lungs for breathing
my existence relies on you
thank you skin
for protecting me from the unseen
thank you bones
for carrying my dreams

'And thank you at the bottom of my eyes
after all the battles you fought
you have never failed to rise

'I apologize for being unkind to you
in the effort to be appreciated by others
I forgot it all starts with: I love you.'

Authenticity

As you bend over limpid water
in your reflection you see
authenticity is when you stop
asking opinions on who you should be

Home

If we make someone else our home
sooner or later, we'll be homeless

But if we make ourselves our home
there's no corner of the world
in which we don't belong
there's no people that are not
our people

Outside the Box

I'm a cloud, don't try to grasp my shape
I grow too fast for you to fit me in a box
By the time you think you have a name for me
the wind will have sculpted me a million times over

Outside the Box II

I'm a book
don't judge me by my cover
on some pages I'm tender
on some pages I'm thunder

Every chapter unmasks a lie
I've been told about
who I'm supposed to be

I got rid of footnotes
to give up on the need
to always justify myself

Gratitude my north star
re-writes an eloquent
acknowledgment session
each and every day

Purpose my faithful companion
ensures that the plot
does not revolve just around me
and includes all the lips
I can lift in a smile

I'm a book
and you may leave a good or bad review
for everyone to see
but you'll never be the same again
after you read the whole of me

The Creative Self

What made you think art is not a real job
when the artist is the human closest to God?
You came to spin along the equator
not to be a consumer, much rather a creator

Instead of pondering, move
ideas will then easily find you
Spend time in nature, under your skin
creating re-affirms the divine within

You say you're not the creative type
and surrender into shrinking
My love, everyone is creative
before they start overthinking

Affirmations

Note to self

They say that it helps to look in the mirror and affirm, 'I am beautiful,' 'I am brave,' 'I am deserving,' 'I am enough,' and the others. But let me remind you that it is okay if you don't yet believe all your affirmations.

Sometimes we must affirm our sacred truths long before we believe them and every day commit to surrendering a little further into them. Eventually, you will stop resisting the realization of the infinite abundance that creates and surrounds you. At last, you will internalize the simple scientific notion that nearly all elements in your body were made in a star, that you are stardust and have nothing left to prove.

Talents

Some talents we keep for ourselves
like unsent letters
gathering dust in old drawers
imagining how little the receiver would care
unaware of how patiently
they are waiting for our message

Service

The impact millionaires
affect the lives of millions

They serve the pain
they want to see removed
and understand
that the truest help
is that which puts others
beyond the need
for further help

The impact millionaires
show up with water
but ask their audience
to bring fertile soil
around their seeds

The impact millionaires elevate
but know that each individual
is their own savior and healer

The impact millionaires
call you to join them
'What is the suffering
you want to alleviate?'

The impact millionaires
all started by impacting
one single person

Who is the person
you can impact today?

Calling

What is my strongest passion?
What is my unique talent?
What does the world need?
How can I sustain myself?
There's a small area in which the answers to these questions overlap.
In this area, I will build my home.

Uniqueness

Why work so hard to create
something out of nothing
when so many others
have already done it
and a million times better
as they are experts
and me just starting?

My attention wanders
to the fingerprint
my inky index left on the paper
a reminder of the unique spark
that no one else can leave
the exact same mark

Strategy

Note to self

The best things in life happen outside of strategic frameworks. You don't need a 5-step plan to be overcome with awe at the sight of a sunset, you can't plan the goosebumps given by an act of kindness, you can't make yourself love someone who checks boxes in your mind but not in your heart.

Strategy is helpful and limiting at once. It aids growth, but it can constrict creativity, spontaneity, and receptiveness to serendipity.

Stop following other people's frameworks. What worked for one won't work for all. If you really want to follow a strategy, let it be one you designed. And on many days, remember to forget it, so life can surprise you with boons you can't yet conceive.

Education

Note to self

Crucial moments in human life occur each time we find out that a belief we held as central to our existence is wrong. In those moments we shatter, and can later use the broken pieces as building blocks for a new more expansive self. This is the liberation that education provides.

Once you identify your passion, become a lifelong student. Learn everything you can about it. Everything you can.

Action

I stood scared of taking the wrong turn
and never reaching and drinking from my well
She said, 'The truth about mistakes is
make many and don't dwell'

Persistence

Achievements pie recipe:
A cup of knowledge
A spoonful of action
An ocean of perseverance

Celebrate Progress

What is a learning curve?
Is it the steep slope
of mountains to climb?
Is it the crest of waves to
swim through on the other side?
Is it the hollow of drops
the tears we have to cry?

It is the jittery curve of your smile
when like a street artist
you learn while everyone watches live

Obstacles

Note to self

Researchers have tried planting trees in an enclosed artificial environment and ensured to include all the necessary variables for the trees' thriving. Yet before even maturing, the trees fell. Why? In this enclosed setting, there was no wind hitting the barks and creating the stress that plants need to stand. To trees, the wind is a stressor and adversity, yet they need it for growth and survival. The same is true for humans. Obstacles thicken our skin.

When obstacles surface on your path, you gain wisdom and maturity, you grow emotionally and intellectually through pain. When obstacles are removed from your path, you gain prosperity and joy, you grow materially and spiritually through insight.

Fierceness

Exit all rooms besides those with matches
that are lit by your same kind of fire
Those mirroring a glimpse of your potential
let them guide you and inspire

Don't pick fights with the narrow-minded
for ignorance is its own punishment
Build a thick armor against the many
who will hammer with discouragement

When they push you towards "safe"
know nothing is safe that doesn't bring peace
When they project their limitations on you
remember they are all based on fears

Defend your dream fiercely
pack compassion and other guns
as if your life depended on it
because it undoubtedly does

Non-Linearity of Progress

I bumped into my shadow
on the way to thorny feelings
she whispered to me:
'You can't rush your healing
Its time is not measured in seconds but steps
some forward, some backward
then forward again'

Non-Linearity of Progress II

What it is to be terrestrial
is for me hard to grasp
some days I move
as if I lived on the moon
my jump covers six meters
I'm a light-minded air balloon

On others my heavy thoughts
make me a creature of Jupiter
where it's hard to be a writer
with gravity so strong
I sweat to lift my arm for long

Consistency

Note to self

So often, creative people are long jumpers who realize mid-air that they'd rather land earlier and jump on another idea than put all their efforts into the flight they already took.

My dear creative self, I know you find delight in your brain's many serendipitous sparks, but you can't always leave things unfinished to chase the next shiny object. You must complete one jump, you must land before you get up again and go on taking another.

My lovely creative self, there's no new beginnings without ends, no perfecting without finishing.

Pain

A dark, gray cloak rests over my skies
carefully stitched by the echo of goodbyes
of plans shattered, expectations defied
of aimless effort, lack of rest and respite

A dark, gray cloak rests over my skies
and it pours with rain from clouds and eyes
mushed dream boxes, ideas untried
I try to log into my hopes, access denied

A hunch from far away suggests that I stop
I could dread every minute, every drop
or rest in knowing it's our fate to see dark times
that behind all clouds, the Sun always shines

A hunch from far away suggests that I breathe
reconnect to the life force I throb with
grasping that pain too drives us to feel alive
that all the rain is there to make our soil fertile

Daily Promises

Monkey Mind Press released a photo book entitled *Self-Betrayal*. It's a compendium of what remains unattainable to those who, like me, have repeated too often, 'You broke my trust' while talking to the mirror.

However, the book comes with solutions at the back. They read, "You can stop betraying yourself by making a promise so small it feels insignificant, a promise impossible to say *no* to. By following through on something tiny, you will rebuild the trust in yourself. You will then gradually add more small promises on your way to accomplishing big projects. How do you think those important undertakings are achieved? By working on them a little bit, every day, over a consistent period."

In other words, *Self-Betrayal* suggests that the reason we can't keep some promises is that they are too big for us to carry at that specific point in time.

The costliest shattered promise I made to myself was the one about writing books. And now this formula was telling me that by writing just a little every day over a consistent time, I could unlock the trust in myself needed to turn the dearest dream into a reality. I didn't quite believe it, but I tried anyway. And I see you are reading this, so I guess it works.

Time Management

Note to self

You're never late. There's no other valid timetable than your internal compass. And I know you often consider yourself good at managing time when you're able to tick off all items on your lengthy to-do list. But what about planning time to take a step back for perspective so you can differentiate what is urgent from what is important?

Schedule silence time, outside the bubble time, time for boredom and creativity, time to catch up with yourself. Often you remain trapped in painful situations simply because you don't take the time to zoom out and re-evaluate. You get so caught up with the work ahead that you forget to glimpse outside of it, far into the horizon, where new solutions and opportunities await. Opportunities to live in alignment with whom you're becoming. Why would you rather live reactively, sleepwalking through your days, than plan date nights with yourself?

The One

My love, take me as a bud
I'm only the promise of a flower
and let us bloom together
holding hands, holding each other

The One II

Note to self

We only see other people through the lens of our conditioning. To know your partner truly, stop projecting on them your expectations based on past traumas, present needs, or future wishes. When you say you dislike their behavior what you are really saying is that you are upset about how they did not meet your expectations and that you would like to control their way of thinking so it fits yours, as if yours were superior.

When you base the relationship on personal expectations and desires, then jealousy, disillusionment, and resentment will emerge. When you feel like you are not getting what you want, you may end up looking outside of the relationship for a new individual to turn into an expectations-fulfilling machine.

If instead of looking outward, you travel deeper within and accept yourself for who you are, you will stop aspiring for perfection in your partner and celebrate their humanness. Embrace your differences, create dialogue to meet halfway not to have it your way. Set boundaries but remove conditions. Praise your partner's daily efforts and acknowledge the child at the bottom of their eyes.

Success

Note to self

Success is a commitment to living in alignment with your core values.

When you borrow other people's ideas of success you make success a destination, something to arrive at. When you borrow ideas of success since they tend to be based on external rewards, you may burn out on the way to achievement and once you obtain the desired object, you realize that it was not worth all the sacrifice. A trick of the mind called *hedonic adaptation* ensures that all extrinsic rewards feel sweet at first before we get used to them and eventually stop appreciating them. Imagine working thirty years to climb a ladder only to find out that the role you sacrificed so much for doesn't bring you purpose or peace. Imagine saving a lifetime to buy a certain car and then getting used to it after a few months when adaptation kicks in.

On the contrary, if you interpret success as a commitment to living in alignment with your core values, then it is not a destination but a journey. It is about the daily decision to remove the dissonance between what you believe and what you actually do. It is about finding the North in things that matter to you more than money and sit at the root of your being. In this scenario, you are successful every single day as you work to take action that avoids internal conflict and opens you up to a sense of contentment. Of course, you can plan to achieve things in the future, but your success never rests on outcomes. It lives in the now.

So let's summarize. Success comes from action that provides intrinsic, not extrinsic rewards. It is a journey, not a destination. It's based on authenticity rather than imitation. It is fuelled by purpose not only by money. It requires becoming comfortable with failure, rather than expecting victory each step of the way.

Like happiness, success can't be chased, as chasing it would be a way of telling ourselves that it is not already with us, that we go through life as walking failures.

Wants *vs* Needs

I aimed for the top of a mountain
so I climbed tirelessly each day anew
I gathered blows and regrets
each step closer to the majestic view

From the summit, I proudly looked down
my home was now higher than most others
but I noticed my neighbors at the top
weren't happier than those in lower quarters

'Why is everyone so serious?' I asked
'A storm is coming and we are closest to the rain'
'But aren't we going to be fine?
Don't we here ask and immediately obtain?'

'Yes, there's an abundance of everything
except for peace and free time
While not valuing others' opinions of you
is regarded as the highest crime'

Here, at the top of the wrong mountain, I learned
that when we overlook gazing within
we chase after what we want, we succeed
only to discover it's not what we need

Wants *vs* Needs II

Note to self

Have you ever considered that some of the things you dream of, you would actually hate if you obtained them? Have you contemplated on how you procrastinate on peace by longing for things for the sole reason that they are not there? Isn't it easy to regret the decisions you didn't take? Yet didn't you also gather moments of joy and awe on your path? And have you taken into account that maybe the things you regret not doing don't weigh heavier than the moments of celebration and wonder you did gather in your life?

Money

Note to self

Money is neither dirt nor God. It is energy. And as you circulate it, you circulate abundance. Neither hoard nor overspend, simply give forward. You can use it to take care of yourself and your loved ones, re-invest it in your purpose and serve others.

Heal your wounds about it and find out that money doesn't intentionally avoid you because you are undeserving nor is it the most relevant asset in your life. Money won't always lack because it did in the past, nor will it always be plentiful because it was in the past.

Money is neither dirt nor God. It is energy for you to circulate.

Social Identity

'I'm a poet,' I concluded
'What does that mean?' the child asked
'I say out loud things that others only
whisper to themselves and then forget'

Social Identity II

If you're a human,
you're made of up to 60% water
unless you're a writer
in which case that's ink

Social Identity III

To the writer, a laptop keyboard is a piano
each tap is a note sent to the reader
for them to add to the melody
with the beat of their heart

Legacy

When my daughters grow up
and look at the trenches
time will have dug on my forehead
I want them to see the wars
other women have fought
so the lines of those after them
wouldn't be trenches, but poems

Purpose

My purpose is to
love being myself
being love itself

My purpose is to
make others feel like a plant
that has just been watered
after they talked to me
or read my words

Purpose II

I dip my pencil in black volcanic sand
to gather the ink of stories untold
of rocks turning into grains
of lava marrying into waves

These mountains won't remember me
even if I smoothed their edges with my feet
I won't remember their names either
nor that of the waves that guided my fleet

Purpose is about interbeing
about how we make others feel and aim
be careful to not mistake this
for people remembering your name

Who Am I?

Note to self

Here you go. After much struggle, you have reconnected to your social identity and your purpose. You have found your way to use your unique talents and passions to serve others. You have gotten to know yourself better and without hesitation in your voice, when asked, 'What do you do?' you have replied, 'I'm a writer.' How wonderful to have finally embraced yourself for who you truly are!

Is this who you truly are though? What happens to the woman who dreams of becoming a world-class surgeon and succeeds but then loses the firmness in her hands? What happens to the man who identifies as a father when he loses his child? What happens to the tennis player who becomes impaired in the mobility of his legs? What happens to the woman who holds on to the identity of "Dan's wife" when Dan divorces her?

Our social identities are subjects to the ebbs and flows of life, they are ever-changing, sometimes meaningful, sometimes meaningless. But if they come and go yet I always stay, then who am I?

Part III – Everything

Halfway

Being and becoming are not
two opposite ends of a highway
they're the left and right guard rails
on the way home
asking us to stay centered

Too much tending
towards one or the other
and we crash

The Breeze

The breeze is nothing but kisses
blown to us by the universe
to tickle the remembrance
of the love for being alive

Expansion

You shrink
victim of a misunderstanding
remember
since the beginning of time
the universe
never stopped expanding

It claims more space
right now
as you read
reclaim more space
right now
as you breathe

Least Effort

Have you seen how flowers
don't try to bloom, they just do?
And how rivers don't try to run
they just go on and move?

Unconcerned as they are
with power, control, or approval
they unfold effortlessly
intuitively, never frugal

When like the rest of nature
we drop the fear of criticism
and act with alignment and love
by doing less, we accomplish more

Pure Potentiality

When a guru tells me
about my infinite creative power
at times I believe it
at others, doubts are louder

But by observing nature
this truth flows strongest
when I glance at a seed
and see a whole forest

Impermanence

The mighty ocean
my dearest guide
teaches wave by wave
that everything comes
and everything goes
in a tireless cosmic tide

Impermanence II

Note to Self

We romanticize "forever." It's the human attempt at creating safety via predictability and continuity. An illusion that is eventually always unmasked. Like when sinking wrinkles and graying hair remind us that no matter how tenaciously we battle against aging, we will grow old anyway.

Those who understand impermanence become comfortable with change, and since life is change, they become comfortable with life. Those who grasp impermanence stop complaining about being too cold or too hot as they know that both are temporary and fleeting.

Instead of seeking changelessness in a world of change, embrace the freedom that comes from change. Plot twists occur even when you're the author, but that's where the magic happens if you don't cling to the old order.

The Storyline

'So you say you're a writer?' the old lady asked to which I nodded proudly.

'And what other superimposed identities do you squeeze yourself into? What other storylines about yourself make you deaf to all criticism or praise that doesn't fit them?' she questioned.

'Well... it took me a long time to embrace this identity of mine. And it gives me a sense of safety and joy,' I tried not to feel offended.

'Good for you!' she exclaimed. 'As long as you are aware that when you feel like your world is falling apart, only your superimposed identity and storyline are actually falling apart.'

'I don't understand,' I traded pride for curiosity.
'Your storyline promises happiness, yet makes you evaluate everything as good or bad. In that evaluation is the source of pain. If you get rid of the storyline, you get rid of the pain. And not just your career-related storyline, all of them,' she claimed.

'So are you suggesting that if something makes me mad, the ultimate solution would be to change the story around it? What if it is not in my power?' I asked her.

Smilingly she continued, 'Not change the story, since you made it up you can drop it completely. An emotion like anger as an automatic response only lasts ninety seconds. When it lasts any longer it is because you choose to fuel it with words and repetitive thoughts. You reinforce that storyline for hours, years, sometimes a lifetime.'

'What shall I do instead?' I thought aloud.
'When the emotion arises, acknowledge it with your full and compassionate attention. Experience it without interpretation. Resist the temptation to tag it as good or bad. Simply be present with it. Investigate where it lives in the body and how it evolves. If you drop the storyline, your emotion won't last longer than one and a half minutes,' she chimed.

Perspective

If life is a test
then the sky is our cheat sheet
when we look up
to the immensity of its blue
we find answers and dreams
pinned for us by the stars

When overwhelmed
take a step back
and gaze up

Detachment

You softly hold a heart
and guard it against all pain
until one day you must
consign it back again

You transit as a pilgrim
and chant your way in hymns
until at the road's end
you must give up your limbs

Worries blot your mind
an ageless ban from heaven
yet fears will leave you too
no thought can last forever

Even the firmest bond
with that dear old friend
one day latest by death
must come to an end

Against prayers and protests
all things move and wane
sharpen your sight today
for nothing stays the same

Don't focus all your efforts
on amassing lands and wells
the only space you need
is the space to be yourself

Giving

In the Middle East lives the Dead Sea
it receives fresh waters from rivers
but doesn't set them free

It takes and takes
without giving a thank
and there before it knows it
its water has gone dank

It doesn't pass it on
its salt levels begin to rise
and conditions are created
that don't support life

You and I too
when we receive without giving
see our waters go dank
our thoughts muddy and unforgiving

When we make it all become
about me, myself, and I
our anxieties soar
discontents multiply

So the easiest door out
of our stagnant salty grief
is to pour ourselves into a river
and selflessly give

Selflessness

Note to Self

Are you interested in others only to the extent in which they enrich and validate your image of yourself? Or do you care about them independently of your own benefit? You may find the answer by evaluating how content you are right now in your life.

Those who suffer the most are the ones who dwell upon themselves and see others as means to their own ends. People who are selflessly interested in others experience a much greater sense of fulfillment.

The arithmetic of selflessness operates by expanding the interest for your welfare into an interest for the welfare of all: It multiplies your joy by the joy of everyone else.

Curiosity

For eons the morning light
strived to pluck all stars away
and trap them in its vase
in a bouquet of Milky Way

Yet every night anew
all stars ran back in place
in the darkest deepest blue
where they belong in space

For years you printed copies
of your dearest expectations
distributed them like flyers
like a party invitation

All those who didn't read them
showed up in cheerful numbers
when the time to dance arrived
they'd left in dreamless slumber

Humans being made of stardust
can't be fooled by verbosity
nor control nor projections
they must be dealt with curiosity

Don't squeeze them into boxes
nor have their freedom tinted
to connect with them deeply
be genuinely interested

Non-Judgement

Overexposed to models of perfection
you judge quickly, create division
like staring at the sun stains your vision

People cast no shadows
when we see in them the divine
inquire instead of trying to define

Oneness

I have VIP seats in a theater
hosting the show of an invisible painter
She strokes a blue canvas with red
helping the sun down a gold windy ladder

In awe I stare at the pinkish shades
that daily rewrite the sky's name
My concerns feel small and insignificant
next to the vastness of the painting's frame

And as I rest against the trunk
of a rainy willow tree
I realize the sunset's painter
is the same that painted me

All the magic I bow to and want to copy
is woven by the same atoms that weave my body
Me, these leaves and those birds in flight
we all merrily bathe in the same sunlight

Another paintbrush paints me a smile
in myriads of shapes, we are externally split
yet looking deeper there's only one thing
and all of us, we all are it

Oneness II

Note to Self

The wise say that nothing dispels grief and fear like the realization of unity: When we override the illusion of separateness and see ourselves in all and all in ourselves.

Physics too remarks that separation only exists as a condition of perception. At the subatomic level, separate phenomena dissolve into a flux of energy. In the world of the senses, unity appears as multiplicity. It appears, but it is not.

Isn't there peace in understanding that you're the sand corn, the snowflake, the acorn, and the fruit fly? Don't you act more lovingly for knowing that there's no "you", only one infinite "I"?

Truth

Note to Self

If we position a daisy in front of a snail and then rapidly snatch it away, the snail will believe that the daisy magically disappeared. This happens because the snail can't detect such fast movement as its nervous system only perceives about three to four images per second. On the contrary, dragonflies see about 300 images a second, at least six times faster than most of us do. We do not know what the external world looks like, all we experience is our own nervous system. Truth transcends the mind and the reasoning we try to experience it with.

Our measurements seem to work at the surface level and never grasp the one thing from which all things are made. We overfocus on details and miss the whole picture. We try to trace why something happens yet cannot find out why a thing is as it is.

The wise suggest that truth is an act of embracing the mystery of what can't be measured but only deeply felt. It is to be wordlessly savored after dropping fears and desires. Truth isn't a science. Truth is a business of the heart.

Wisdom

In the middle of the night
when the deepest dark awakens
wisdom comes in the form of riddles
it can't be given, only taken

It is awareness of your feelings
the choice of now instead of later
the act of resting in existence
an unmasking the mind-jailer

Where knowledge teaches us
how to live life on our terms
wisdom reminds us
life is lived on nature's terms

That selfless giving births a joy
grander than prizes and above
that the ultimate form of wisdom
is unconditional love

Abundance

A thump-thump that never forgets
to drum the tune of life in your chest
that doesn't rely on you remembering
to pump your lungs with new breaths

The balmy hand of nature
showing the way at night
when dewdrops burn like torches
to guide you with moonlight

The gift of the sacred power
to infinitely tweak your mindset
you can't hit snooze on a sunrise
you can hit reset on a sunset

Ignore the paradigm of scarcity
designed to make you consume more
know that in your search for abundance
you are what you're searching for

Acceptance

The volcano bursts
molten rock from Earth's core
flow of incandescent demolition
it spares nothing
not the farms
not the houses
not the roads
not the people
The volcano destroys

The volcano bursts
molten rock from Earth's core
flow of dazzling conception
it designs everything
new landscapes
new mountains
new islands
new fertile soil
The volcano creates

A Big Bang
of creation from destruction
Don't fight it
you are the volcano

Love

'Mom, what is love?'
'When someone responds
to the joys and sorrows of others
as if they were their own'

'But what does it look like?'
'Dropping a worm in a small beak
watering plants, offering help
without expecting a win'

'And what does it feel like?'
'A bridge crossing an abyss
breeze under scorching sun
the ultimate form of bliss'

'And where is it to find?'
'From love comes all we do
like desire is love of the self
knowledge is love of truth'

'Mom, how can I love more?
And how can it be weighed?'
'My dear, you are love itself
when you're not afraid'

Love II

To annihilate distances
exhale love in the gaps
between the stars
and watch the universe shrink
into a marble so tiny
it fits in the left pocket
of your heart

Gifts

I'll give you fireflies on your birthday
because the best gift is to remind someone
of the light that shines within them

Softness

Keep your heart soft
a hard heart breaks when it falls
a soft one bounces back in the chest
it hurts
but it doesn't shatter

Meditation

I stand in a boxing ring and clutch
I can't wear boxing gloves
thumb and index finger must touch
I adjust my mouthguard
focus to get aligned
let me introduce my opponent
the famous monkey mind

I begin overthinking my strategy
Do I repeat mantras
or watch my breath's pace?
Do I scan my body
or let it dissolve in space?

By the time I've counted two breaths
she's already hit me with her scripts
and monkey being a pro director
drama abounds in her clips

Then suddenly a deeper breath from the belly
gathers my attention, the outbreath is freeing
I feel everything and nothing
I feel the graciousness of being

It is only one instant before my opponent
hits me again with her right hook
and mind wandering begins anew
diligently writing its pessimistic book

Sometimes the breath
is louder than the noise
more often it's the monkey
that lets me hear her voice

Until I realize that opposing
is not what she's about

I can observe where she takes me
and go back to here and now

When victory is announced
I admit I am surprised
as I am proclaimed the winner
because today again I tried

Meditation II

Note to Self

Minds are grasshoppers jumping from worry to worry. They place their focus on the outer world and filter it in problems. They see separation in place of unity and incompleteness in place of wholeness.

Meditation helps the hoppers turn their attention to the inner life of their thoughts and feelings and become aware of their negative patterns. In that awareness, the hoppers realize that solving problems is not about rearranging things outside. Solving problems is about letting go of the patterns that make them filter life in problems.

Meditation trains the hoppers to observe instead of mindlessly reacting to adversity and challenge. They realize that many of their desires are not choices but compulsions turned into conditioned habits and that these do not serve them or the people around them.

In meditation, the hoppers stop hopping and begin resting in existence.

Happiness

I rubbed my sleepy eyes and the park appeared and disappeared under the weight of my fingers on the lids. I turned towards the fountain and spotted a female silhouette in the water. What was a grown-up doing showering fully clothed under the park's little spring? My pupils sprang open with excitement as I recognized the female figure to be Lady Happiness herself.

I ran to the water and tried to claim her attention in every way. I danced, I sang, I made offerings, I ate, I spoke of love, I confided, I worked hard, but all in vain. Lady Happiness seemed deaf to my calling. Only when I stopped trying to attract her, she came to rest by my side.

'Ma'am, I am overjoyed that You honor me with Your presence. What can I do to see more of You?'
'Why do you buzz like a fly against a window?' she asked back sternly.
'Ma'am, I do not understand.'
'You buzz and buzz, chasing the illusion of the view outside. You're so busy buzzing that you don't notice the window has been open all along.'
'Ma'am, I apologize if I offended You. I only wanted to know how You feel, and what I can do to keep You by my side. And You seem very serious, maybe I have...'
'You expected me to be a giddy being, breathing out rainbows and humming joyful songs.'
'Well, yes Ma'am. Now that You mention it, I expected some vivaciousness.'
'Have you ever considered that I may not be giddiness but calmness, the feeling of homecoming even in the midst of a storm? Have you ever seen me as the part of you that remains steady through joys and sorrows, the anchor to the deepest roots of your being?'

Then Lady Happiness left me, so I could ponder over her nature.

Death

Gray hair after gray hair
our unmaking is unfurled
our parents sent us to death
bringing us into the world

Gray hair after gray hair
and we try to pull it out
until pulling all gray hair
would leave us quite without

Gray hair after gray hair
walking feels as if through snow
heavy limbs and lighter heart
our last steps in the unknown

Death awaits like road shimmer
final reaching of a shore
once we drive over it
it is not there anymore

God

A stray cat startles me
with its opalescent eyes

tree branches so barren
still reaching for the skies

mountains moved by clouds
disappear in white disguise

the hollow of a beggar's hands
a child gasping in surprise

inside of all but ideologies
there is where my God lays

Purpose – Revisited

Note to Self

You spend so much time trying to figure out your life's purpose. That's because you are confused about who you are. You think you have a life and forget that you are life. And life only is in the now.

It follows that your entire life's purpose is whatever you're doing right now. When you're watching a sunset, that's your life's purpose. When you're working on a project, that's your life's purpose. When you're eating, that's your life's purpose.

Since life is only ever happening here and now, if you think your life's purpose is something outside of right now, you'll miss your entire life.

Wonder

We walk on waters
but it's not a miracle
we skim life's surface so lightly
our sleepwalking is literal

We miss out on sunsets
though their poetry is lyrical
we are trapped in distractions
their net often digital

Contentment abounds
not in the minds who ponder
but in the eyes of those
who look at the world
in a state of perpetual wonder

Freedom

When you like what's sweet
and dislike what's bitter
you are not free
you're a victim

of your thoughts and desires
the more control you win over them
the less manipulated by lies

To be free stop looking at yourself
through someone else's eyes
to be free practice forgiveness
right then when anger arises

To be free schedule time
with nothing scheduled but being alive
to be free move your couch
to face a sunset, not a TV pantomime

Freedom is not
always doing what one likes
it's cultivating the lightness
to willingly do what's right

Who Am I?

Note to Self

I have learned that I am not my feelings, I am not a social role, I am not a superimposed identity, I am not a personal brand, I am not time, I am not space. I can perceive all those things, which means I'm not them. I am the observer, the awareness that perceives. When they evolve and progress and wane, I watch them evolve and progress and wane.

However, this didn't seem a satisfactory answer. So I went to my guru and asked, 'Who am I?' He told me to inquire within and meditate on it. A few months later, I returned to my guru and said, 'I still have not found who I am.' He suggested that I continue meditating on it.

I kept meditating on the 'Who am I?' and nothing came. Tired by the aimless effort, I went back to my teacher to protest and inquire. He smiled, 'The question will not be answered. It will simply dissolve once the "I" dissolves. As the "I" shrinks, the answer opens. As the ego shrinks, you encounter your true being. Then for the first time, you can truly surrender.'

'How am I to surrender?' I kept asking.

My teacher answered, 'The ego is a mountain. Height is the ego's main concern. The ego wants to climb, reach above others. Surrender, on the other hand, is an ocean, a depth. When the ego shrinks there is no wish to be above, you are the one that is all. There's no wish to be the tallest wave, you are the whole ocean. When the ego shrinks, you are everything.'

Acknowledgments

This book finds its foundation in the work of my parents. I thank my mother for modeling the art of love and my father for modeling the art of living authentically and pursuing one's dreams. I thank dad for the work on the book cover too, which represents for me an epitome of his teachings while serendipitously encompassing the spirit of this book. I thank my brother, for his ways are constant reminders of the gentleness and kindness one can choose to go through life with.

Immense gratitude goes to my editor, Advyth Herur, for his insightful and witty suggestions, the patience with which he helped me create more consistency and simplicity, and the many thought-provoking side notes.

Importantly, this manuscript wouldn't exist without the lessons gathered from my many mentors. Behind my words hides the inspiration elicited by the work of Deepak Chopra, Brendon Burchard, Michael Beckwith, Pema Chodron, Eknath Easwaran, Jay Shetty, Yung Pueblo, Eckhart Tolle, Nicole LePera, Alexandra Michelle, and several others.

Finally, special thanks go to the child at the bottom of my eyes for her unwavering faith, for providing direction and purpose, and for insisting that I share these words so they could tickle the child at the bottom of yours.

About the Author

Valentina Quarta was born and raised in a small village in the south of Italy. She left Italy in her early twenties to live in several other European countries. Illness and a sense of unfulfillment motivated her to embark on a self-discovery journey. She graduated in literature first, psychology later, and began combining the two worlds in her writings.

For the past years, she has been inspiring self-awareness and transformation for thousands of followers on social media.

Connect with Valentina on Instagram, TikTok, and Insight Timer, or send her an email at valentinathewriter@gmail.com

Table of Contents

Part I – Nothing

Beginnings 3
The Body 4
Receiving 5
Vicious Cycles 6
Uncoupling 7
Belonging 8
Narratives 9
Burnout 10
Worthiness 11
Navigation 12
Procrastination 13
Self-Doubt 14
Northless 15
Imposter Syndrome 16
The Ego 17
Paper Dad 18
Shadow Selves 19
Loneliness 20
The Waiting Room 21
Anxieties 22
No Screens Attached 23
Avoidance 24
The Clock 25
Who Am I? 26

Part II - Something

Potential 31
Passion 32
The Power of Yet 33
Courage 34
Renewal 35
Awareness 36
Un-Layering 37
Excuses 38
Beliefs 39
Attention 40

Pacing 41
Essentialism 42
Resilience 43
Resilience II 44
Mindfulness 45
Presence 46
Gratitude 47
Journaling 48
Vulnerable Self-Talk 49
Connection 50
Beauty 51
Heritage 52
Direction 53
Direction II 54
The Unknown 55
The Unknown II 56
The Truth about Fear 57
The Truth about Fear II 58
The Truth about Fear III 59
Meaning 60
Self-Love 61
Self-love II 62
Compassion 63
Patience 64
Forgiveness 65
Forgiveness II 66
Negative Emotions 67
Failure 68
Strength 69
Quitting 70
Flow 71
Comparison 72
Authenticity 75
Home 76
Outside the Box 77
Outside the Box II 78
The Creative Self 79
Affirmations 80
Talents 81
Service 82
Calling 83
Uniqueness 84

Strategy 85
Education 86
Action 87
Persistence 88
Celebrate Progress 89
Obstacles 90
Fierceness 91
Non-Linearity of Progress 92
Non-Linearity of Progress II 93
Consistency 94
Pain 95
Daily Promises 96
Time Management 97
The One 98
The One II 99
Success 100
Wants vs Needs 102
Wants vs Needs II 103
Money 104
Social Identity 105
Social Identity II 106
Social Identity III 107
Legacy 108
Purpose 109
Purpose II 110
Who Am I? 111

Part III - Everything

Halfway 115
The Breeze 116
Expansion 117
Least Effort 118
Pure Potentiality 119
Impermanence 120
Impermanence II 121
The Storyline 122
Perspective 123
Detachment 124
Giving 125
Selflessness 126
Curiosity 127

Non-Judgement 128
Oneness 129
Oneness II 130
Truth 131
Wisdom 132
Abundance 133
Acceptance 134
Love 135
Love II 136
Gifts 137
Softness 138
Meditation 139
Meditation II 141
Happiness 142
Death 143
God 144
Purpose - Revisited 145
Wonder 146
Freedom 147
Who Am I? 148

Acknowledgments 151

About the Author 153

Before you go…

Dearest reader,

The author invites you to leave a review and let her know how you felt along this ride from nothing to something to everything. Since reviews support the discoverability of the book, your commentary will help a fellow human find their way to these words and the author in her mission to spread this message of awareness and purpose.

Reviews may be written on Amazon, Goodreads, Barnes & Nobles, et al.

Much gratitude and love in advance for your contribution!

Manufactured by Amazon.ca
Bolton, ON